THE JOYS OF MOTHERHOOD

**To Andy,
who taught us the joys**

Library of Congress Catalog Card Number: 87-71163
ISBN: 0-8362-2097-8

First Printing, August 1987
Fourth Printing, April 1991

THE JOYS OF MOTHERHOOD

by Barbara & Jim Dale

Andrews and McMeel
A Universal Press Syndicate Company
Kansas City • New York

Well, here we are, you and me. Mothers. Can you believe it?
MOTHERS!!!

Wasn't it about two weeks ago that we were in high school
whispering in the halls about how far you should let a guy go with
you when you're not sure if you're really in love with him but he is
pretty cool and every girl you know would die to go out with him?

Now we have children. Little miniature humans who rely on us to
be responsible and level-headed and all those other things our
mothers kept telling us we weren't.

Children!!! You can't return them or put them on layaway. This is
strictly all sales final.

Remember when we said, no way? I do. We swore to each other we wouldn't get caught in that suburban, middle-class, diapers and doctors, "What kind of formula do you use?" you-can't-find-a-baby-sitter-when-you-need-one, HE never helps with anything, RUT.

So, welcome to the rut. One day your period doesn't come and the next day the dress size you achieved only by a lifetime of refusing to eat during months that end in y is nothing but a fast-fading memory. "Honest, I was a size six, just like Cheryl Ladd. Stop giggling or I'll pin you against the wall with my belly."

Sorry, I gotta run or I'll be off schedule. It's time for tiptoeing over to the crib during the baby's nap and staring in, reduced to a quivering, mushy fool by the curled up little ball of a person that I actually made.

Hi again, is it a bad time? Is there a good time?

You know what I was thinking about the other day? There was a distinct time in our lives when we started doing things that we can't rationally explain. Really. Like when you're pregnant. And you go out and actually sign up for a class that teaches you how to breathe. (You probably thought you already knew how.) And in the same class they teach us that the excruciating pain of having a cruise ship launched from between one's thighs doesn't really hurt at all.

And talking about rational . . . how about morning sickness? Hah! We won't get morning sickness. Not us. It's only in movies and your imagination and Oops-I-gotta-run-to-the-bathrooooooom!!!

But then, right about the time you get to be so big that you have to look at other people's feet just to remember what feet look like and so immobile that you think somebody's going to put Ficus benjamina around you and call you the Human Planter, just about the time you become totally ambidextrous with a fork—the miracle comes.

The miracle of pain. HOW CAN ANYTHING HURT THAT MUCH??? We said we'd find husbands who were understanding and enlightened and helpful and THEY'RE THE SWINE WHO GOT US INTO THIS TORTURE!!! The doctor asks if you have the urge to push. The urge to push? How about the DEMAND TO EXPLODE? Who is he kidding? Gimme a bullet to bite.

Lamaze . . . that's French for, "If you believe labor can be painless, I'd like to show you some land in Wyoming." Natural childbirth, they call it. Let's not forget that the Ice Age, bee stings, and PMS are all natural. And the spinal, along with the VCR, hot fudge, and microwave ovens, are all artificial. You tell me, which group has been better to you?

Oh . . . oh . . . oh, my God. It's beautiful. Life. Wet and pink and tiny and wondering where everything is and not having any pockets to keep things in. My baby.

Uh-oh, I never should've said the word "baby" out loud. Mine just heard me. It's time for a bottle or a breast or a pacifier—God, they suck a lot.

I'll call you on my next sanity break.

SOMEDAY I'M SURE WE'LL CHUCKLE OVER THIS AS ONE OF THOSE CUTE ANECDOTES FROM YOUR CHILDHOOD, BUT IN THE MEANTIME I THINK I'LL JUST YELL AND SCREAM AND LOSE CONTROL OF MYSELF.

DEAR, I HAVE GOOD NEWS AND BAD NEWS
ABOUT ANDY. FIRST, I THINK HE WANTS
TO GROW UP TO BE A DOCTOR. SECOND,
HE'S ALREADY PRACTICING ON THE
LITTLE GIRL ACROSS THE STREET.

Hello. It's me. You were sleeping? Oh, I'm so sorry, I shattered a religious experience.

Just think, in college we used to sleep until we woke up. Nine hours. Fourteen hours. Some people became semi-famous for sleeping so much they missed entire days of the week. We used to hang around at their doors and observe them like exhibits at the Museum of Natural History. Sominus Humanus.

Now sleep is like wild truffles. You can hardly find it. When you do, there's never enough of it. You always want more. Some people have it and don't even appreciate it and you want theirs.

Wah! It's 3 A.M. Infant Standard Time.

Did you ever think you could get up and walk and fill a bottle and change a diaper and powder a bottom and sing a song and rock in a rocker without being legally awake? Did you ever think you could do it for three months straight?

Of course, then any spare moment becomes S.P. —Sleep Potential. Right? Right? What's that noise? You're snoring. Okay, listen to what I say. Very carefully place the receiver in the top drawer of the desk so no one can call you, then walk to the sofa, lie down and I'll talk to you when we've both recovered. Bye.

It's time to get up. But I'm having a great dream. The kids actually take care of themselves. They make their own lunches. They clean up. They do their homework. No measles, no chicken pox. No acne! I have leisure time. My car doesn't have gum all over it. It's peaceful in the house. My husband and I take long quiet walks.

Uh-oh. The dream is almost over. Pretty soon I'll have to face the real world. Gotta open my eyes. Here goes. You can do it.

<u>Another Day Begins</u> !!!

Hi there. Guess who? How are you holding up? Don't give up. Only seventeen more years to go.

Hey, isn't it adorable the way children repeat everything we say? "Da-da." "Ma-ma." "Go sleepy now." "Bye-bye." "Tell story." "Want dinner." "Aunt Lucille is a fat pig."

<u>WARNING: THIS IS A TODDLER LEARN-TO-WALK ALERT.</u>
This is not a drill. Repeat, this is not a drill.
—Place any object you wish to see whole again
above Grabbing Level—

Well, so we've stayed home for the last four years, prisoners of a child czar, reduced to waiter-cook-valet-chauffeur-nurse-slave-serf-menial, watching "Sesame Street," "Mr. Rogers," and "The Electric Company," communicating in a vocabulary composed of nursery rhymes, fables, and phrases like "make poo-poo." And we've dreamed of freedom, POWs caught behind enemy playpens. And then, when the day finally comes—O, Nursery School, thy savior—then what do we do?

Of course, we weep. "My baby's gone! My poor baby! Alone! Not to return. For three whole hours!"

Followed, three and a half hours later by, "I can't wait till tomorrow."

Oh, it's your day to drive. Fun, huh?

By the way, the car pool was invented by a sociologist who didn't believe in the death penalty but wanted to find a punishment that's even worse. Hell on Wheels. "The accused is found guilty and is hereby sentenced to life in a station wagon with small sticky people."

Talk to you later. . . .

So . . . what's new?

We just got back from a Little League game. 43 to 3. That's more runs than we scored all last season . . . 3.

Wait till your first game. Just be sure to remember all those articles we've read by those mellow '60s shrinks who speak in Librium-calm voices saying:

Thou shalt never dwell on competition, only the spirit of sportsmanship.
Thou shalt never shout out negative commentary, only positive reinforcement.
Thou shalt never concentrate on scores and winning, but only on the joy of the game.

And then when you get to the game . . .

"SAFE??? THAT LITTLE CREEP WAS OUT BY A MILE, YOU FOUR-EYED BOZO!!!! HOW MUCH ARE THEY PAYING YOU TO THROW THE GAME???"

By the way, the parent-teacher conference is Tuesday at 11:30.

You probably noticed they ask you what time you'd like and then no matter what time you ask for, they tell you it's already taken until finally you ask them what time you can have and they give you a choice of two times that are either the one and only dentist appointment you could get in this decade or that private, quiet bath you had put on your calendar last May. So you flip a coin and your teeth win and your sanity in the bathtub loses.

Anyway, the conferences are important. To me at least. I have to find out how I'm doing. Did I get all those fractions right? And how did she like the way I colored in all the countries in the Western Hemisphere? I had your teacher last year. She's tough. We had to do a lot of assignments over.

Which reminds me . . . both of us should feel pretty ridiculous now about shopping so long for those "Hawaiian Macadamia Beige" colored refrigerators. I mean, when was the last time you saw the "Hawaiian Macadamia Beige" color since the whole front of the refrigerator got covered in school papers-with-shiny-little-red-stars and pastel chalk art projects-that-rub-off-on-your-fingers and weekly lunch menus (the exact same stuff *we* had) and Monday-Wednesday-Fridays-you-drive-mornings, Tuesday-Thursdays-you-pick-up, except every-third-week-when-everything-reverses car pools, and doctors' appointments and birthday parties and recitals and lessons and reminders and permission slips (Has *anyone* ever sent a permission slip back to school that said, "No, I refuse to let Willard go to the historical museum and learn something valuable. I'd rather he stay back and stare at the gerbil on his treadmill."). Anyway, so much for "Hawaiian Macadamia Beige."

Oh, I almost forgot to tell you. There is a way to get baseball card bubble gum out of pantyhose. You wash the pantyhose in vinegar. The bad part is, you smell like a salad.

Okay. It's time to take mental stability inventory. How are we doing? What was the last movie you saw? Anything that stars a puppet doesn't count. How about books you've read? To *yourself*! Are you still eating the scraps of food they leave on their plates? I finally quit. Self-hypnosis. I convinced myself I was no better than a bag lady who works indoors.

Face it, we need a break. Not often. Say, once every eight years. We take fifteen minutes and just say, "Hey, this is for us." Let people call us selfish, I don't care if you don't.

Enough rambling. A dog just came in the house. I know we don't have a dog. At least we didn't until twenty seconds ago. He's licking me. I hate it when nonhumans lick.

Until the next Fun Report . . .

Sugared cereal.

44

Hi there, bright eyes.

Say, I hate to start the morning off with a quiz but something has been bothering me. Is this stuff we're putting in their lunches really food? Rolled up sheets of fruit-flavored rubber that look suspiciously like wallpaper. Juice that comes in triangular aluminum envelopes—are you supposed to drink it or mail it? Pudding that *brags* about never having been put in a refrigerator. It's all a little too George and Jane Jetson for me.

Anyway, it was nice seeing you two the other night. Being out just like people. I notice you have the same habit I do. Automatically wiping the mouth of the person next to you. Whoever that man was, he never even said thanks.

I understand, some patterns are hard to break. Like when you scraped and stacked all the dishes for the busboy. But telling the waiter we couldn't have dessert because of the "bad job" we did on our vegetables was a little embarrassing.

But really, let's do it more often. I don't know about you, but I need a glimpse of the real world now and then. Isn't it amazing how many GROWNUPS are out there? People without bibs, rubber pants, jelly on their cheeks, bicycle bruises, missing front teeth, or strep throats.

By the way, speaking of getting out . . . your baby-sitter called me for a reference on you. She wanted to know how many phones you have, if you have either a VCR or cable or both, what kinds of leftovers you leave in the refrigerator, how good your stereo is, what you pay per hour, how much you tip, what you'll pay when you REALLY need a sitter, and how good your decorating taste is in case her boyfriend comes by. On her 10-point rating system, you scored an 8.6.

Uh-oh, I gotta go. A small boy just walked into my house, hugged me, and went to the cupboard for a cookie. It doesn't bother me that I've never seen this child before. I just wonder how he knew where the cookies were. . . .

50

Hello, did you notice? It happened yesterday . . . when we weren't looking. We got old!!!

Okay, it's one thing to be a mother. Responsible. Reliable. All that stuff. But suddenly we're O.P.—Old People. We're—are you ready?—a different generation!

The kids snicker and whisper and ask you those questions. "Do you remember Kennedy?" "Did you ever listen to the Beaties?" "What did you eat before yogurt?"

Admit it. You get tired easily, don't you? Once in a while you catch yourself content to just stare out the window. And sometimes you "ache." Remember when you thought you'd never use that word. It's so decrepit. "Aaaache."

And have you noticed, people are more polite to you. Like if they bump into you with their shopping cart it's, "Oh, I'm so sorry, did I hurt you, can I help you, are you all right, is everything okay, do you bruise easily, are you going to expire right here in the frozen food aisle???"

I was out in the yard the other day and one of the neighborhood kids asked if I still knew how to ride a bike. I don't think his mother heard what I called him.

You too? They throw the ball to you underhand now?

Well, the whole thing is ridiculous. We're no different than we were last year or the year before. I can do whatever I want. And I can sure keep up with these kids. So can you. Sure we can. No problem.

I mean, look at all these activities they've got. And we can handle all of them, right?

Piano lessons, swimming classes, roller skating. Big deal. Scout meetings, soccer league, baseball. No sweat. Gymnastics, hockey, karate. Well . . . I don't know about you but between the standing body back-flips and the "Oriental Kill Kick" I do get a little—what's the word—"aaaachey."

I think I better go and soak for a while.

"I THINK I'M FINALLY BEGINNING
TO UNDERSTAND YOUR DECISION."

If you have a boy, you have to know about "guys". There are Star Wars guys... Masters of the Universe guys... GI Joe guys... Black Star guys... Dungeons and Dragons guys... Super Friends guys... There is no such thing as too many guys. There <u>are</u> a few girls which explains how come there are so many guys — at night they multiply.

This is a simple arrangement just between us.
You get the cake and you never, _repeat_ _never_,
reveal the number you saw when Mommy
was on the bathroom scale.

Hello and welcome to Endless Clothes Shopping. I'll pick you up at 3:30 so they'll have almost another full day of growing done before we buy anything new.

Sometimes I have nightmares that this is really a horror movie—

THE CHILD WHO WOULDN'T STOP GROWING!!!

He came from normal parents but his feet grew an inch between breakfast and lunch.
He fell asleep in pajamas that fit but woke up in shrunken rags.
Department stores sent me thank-you notes.
We had to enlarge his room so his legs would fit in.

Do you think we'd be considered cruel if we tried feeding them less for a month or so to see if it would slow down their growth rate? It works with plants. Come to think of it, maybe we should just keep them out of sunlight. I swear mine grow so fast that we have a pair of shoes that got to be too small between the time the right one got tied and the left one got put on. I have one never-used left sneaker.

Speaking of sneakers, we have Learning to Ride a Bike Torture today. You know, where you run alongside the bike as fast as possible, holding onto the seat while a miniature driver shouts, "Don't-let-go-don't-let-go-don't-let-go" and drags his or her sneakers along the ground for brakes, thereby making it impossible to build up enough speed to actually ride and simultaneously destroying a pair of sneakers so new the charge hasn't even revolved once.

That reminds me. Do you have any extra bandages? Every time we have Bike Torture there's a lot of knee and elbow bleeding. Mine. From caroming off garage walls and garbage cans. And I feel foolish wearing those bandages with superheroes and convertible robots on them.

I'll let you go. I know your mother's coming soon. Talk about a mixed blessing. They're the only people in the world who really understand us but they never come without their Master's Degree in Advice. "Have you . . . ? Did you . . . ? Will you . . . ? Why don't you . . . ? How about . . . ? You should . . . ! You must . . . ! You better . . . !"

Even though you say you hate your sister, you really love your sister because she's your sister and it just SEEMS like you hate her and you really WOULD hate her if she WASN'T your sister, but since she IS, you DON'T. Understand?

Hi. Okay, I confess, I'm doing it too. They just seem to slip out. You know, they fit the situation so well. And there's one for everything that happens.

THE PARENTAL CLICHÉ

Go to your room.
Wait till your father gets home.
How many times do I have to tell you?
I don't care what *his* mother says, I say . . .
Don't make me repeat myself.
I'm going to count to three.
Because I said so.
Don't talk back to me.
When I was your age . . .
Where did you ever hear language like that?
How come you couldn't act like ———? He/She listens
    to his/her mother.
If he jumped off a building, would you?
Sit up.
Sit down.
Sit still.
You're grounded.

It's like the universal language of parents. And it never dies. Centuries from now people will have progressed in every way except they'll still discipline their children with the exact same phrases. In other countries they say this stuff only in foreign languages. I'll bet you they say, "Wait till your father gets home" in Peru.

Somebody must have first invented these clichés. Imagine. All these mothers real frustrated with their kids and no standard all-purpose comebacks.

Then all of a sudden, one mother comes along and says, "Go to your room" and a hush falls over the parental world. Wow! The illogical, dictatorial, don't argue with me, LAW! There must be more. And sure enough, this genius mother comes up with a whole string of them. Her words are immortal, more popular than Shakespeare. She's the greatest writer of all time and we don't even know her name. I think *every* year at this time we should take a minute or two and say a silent thank-you to Mrs. Cliché. Without her we wouldn't be able to answer virtually any problem with "Because I said so."

Uh-oh, gotta run and I mean *now*! We've got some big trouble here. But I'm not worried. I'll just use "I'm going to count to three." I haven't used it since Tuesday. Bye for now.

DO YOU SOLEMNLY SWEAR TO EAT YOUR ENTIRE HAM SANDWICH **AND** YOUR CARROT STICKS <u>BEFORE</u> YOU TOUCH YOUR FUDGIE-WUDGIE BAR?

Hi there, Sunshine.

I don't know, I guess I've caught a little Summer Spirit.

You know what I like best about summer vacations? Nothing. As in, "Mom, I have nothing to do."

Oh, really? Perhaps you'd consider playing with the $76,000 worth of toys and sports equipment and other entertainment items we've purchased for you over the past couple of years. Or, God forbid, maybe you'd venture OUTDOORS for an hour or two. Or—better sit down for this one—maybe you could (*whisper*) help me with a few things around the house.

I think I've figured out what children consider "something" to do. First, it has to be inside. Second, you have to be air-conditioned while you do it. Third, food should be handy. Fourth, it should require absolutely no brain activity. So, what does it include? Go ahead, guess.

You got all three on the first shot:
    Going to the mall.
    Video games.
    Destruction movies.

You know what the best part of summer vacation is? Right! When it's over. Back to school. As soon as August comes, I have dreams at night of getting up the next morning and seeing that school bus arrive and taking presents out to the driver.

You've had that dream? Oh, in yours there's a news bulletin on TV announcing that due to a national protest by parents, school will be starting two months early this year? Great fantasy.

But really, we're being too harsh. I used to like having a little one around the house.

THAT'S IT! A little "one." Whose idea was it to have more than one? Who spread that vicious rumor that an only child will grow up to be a social misfit . . . and what's so wrong with social misfits anyway? I wanted to have children, I admit. But I never recall any desire to raise a troop. To run a hotel. To have feeding time in place of meals. To hose down rooms. To do industrial-size laundry loads. To buy only the Giganto Econo-Bargain Multi-Serve Size. To select a car on the basis of interior cubic feet.

But . . . too late. We have our litter. And personally, I have to go and fill their troughs. Call you after we send 'em to the bunkhouse tonight.

I DON'T LIKE YOU TO TALK TO ME LIKE THAT.

I DON'T LIKE YOU TO LEAVE YOUR ROOM SUCH A MESS.

I DON'T LIKE YOUR FRIENDS HANGING AROUND ALL DAY.

AND I ESPECIALLY DON'T LIKE THE FACT THAT YOU'RE TALLER THAN ME.

Hello and Help!!!

They're growing up. Did you see the last batch of school pictures? Combed hair. No unidentified gorp on the clothing. Girls with pouting lips.

The boys have stopped hitting the girls and the girls are less than a foot taller than the boys.

Just for the record, we've surrendered the use of our telephone. You know the little holey thing you hear out of on the phone? Well, I saw that exact imprint on one of the kids' ears. Plus I swear I've seen their hands involuntarily clench into the "receiver cradling position."

And have you heard the conversations?

> "And then he like went up to her and said like 'Oh sure' and she said—are you ready—'I like don't care.' Can you believe she like doesn't care? I don't. You do???? Yuck! Puke! Are you going you-know-where, you-know-when, cuz you-know-who *might* be there. I'm like not and that's like for sure. Okay, maybe. God, that English teacher is like so disgusting. Cute??? V-O-M-I-T."

I wonder if Alexander Graham Bell had kids. I can just see him trying to demonstrate his new invention to the reporters, pacing back and forth waiting for his daughter to hang up.

I notice you have "call waiting." Now your kids can talk to two friends at once. And twice as many people can't get through to us.

Do you eavesdrop? Admit it. Me too. You walk sort of slowly through the room when they're talking and see what you can find out, right? It's like a soap opera right in your own home. "The Young and the Sloppy."

I know, the whole thing just makes you feel old. Going steady . . .
we just got past that ourselves, didn't we? And worrying about
which sweater to wear in case *he* looks at you . . . that was just last
week, I'm sure. I'm too young to be a mother, I still *need* one of
my own.

Call you back when I grow up.

Hi. I got your message. I can't believe it.

Take the car???!!!!
And drive it????!!!!!!

They're children. Babies. They can barely see over the wheel. And they drive with one hand permanently stuck to the radio. Punching those little buttons incessantly, in mid-song, in mid-sentence, mid-word. While the other hand is beating out the rhythm of these millisecond songs on the steering wheel. What I want to know is, which hand is driving?

I saw your car go by a little while ago. I had no idea it could hold that many people.

Those car insurance costs are a joy, aren't they? A moonshot is a lower risk. I can't say that I disagree. Who would you rather trust? An Air Force All-American with Perfect Teeth . . . or an adolescent with green and blue hair, one Molly-bolt earring, a spiked belt, a torn shirt with the message "Eat Live Rhinos," lurching and twitching when he walks because he has headphones permanently implanted in his ears, who is about to take off in a car that costs more than your first house did?

I've figured out an intelligent way to deal with it. Ignore it. And change the subject.

For instance, you think about pleasant things like the person they're dating . . . or whatever they call their mating ritual. It should be renamed Standing Around With A Blank Look On Your Face With A Person Of The Opposite Sex. Oh no, I swore I wouldn't mention the word "sex." Sorry.

Well, did you have your "talk" yet? It's not as bad as it seems. Once you settle down, relax, and start to talk honestly with each other, you realize they know much more about "it" than you do and you just hope to pick up a few pointers.

You're right, we do have to just laugh at some of this stuff. It's not the end of the world. What the heck. Laugh a little. Ha. That's about enough.

Time to go back to a natural state of panic. Personally I think Chastity Belts for Teenagers have gotten a bad rap for too long.

What's that? Sure, talk to you later. I'd hang up too if my car came back a different color than it left.

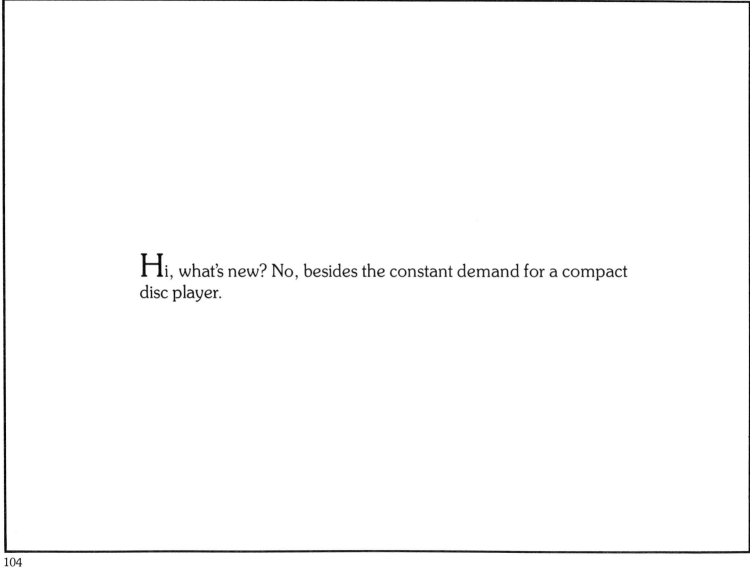

Hi, what's new? No, besides the constant demand for a compact disc player.

You what? You did? You went in? You touched things?

You're braver than I am. Teenagers' rooms were not meant to be visited by adults . . . except maybe anthropologists studying adolescent mold. Are you feeling feverish? Have you noticed any bacteria on your fingertips? Was there a piece of pizza stuck to your shoe? Here's the big question: Did you spot any living things? You know, snakes, frogs, mice, gerbils, furry insects, or maybe one of those slimy gurgling blobs that make the cover of those newspapers at the supermarket. . . .

"FROTHING GREEN MASS SWALLOWS ENTIRE FAMILY IN BISMARCK, NORTH DAKOTA"

What made you go in there? Oh, yeah, it is a problem when you get down to only three plates in your whole set of dishes. What did you find once you went in? Really? A stuffed and mounted marlin. A snow shovel. Eggs??? Yeah, I bet they would give off an aroma. You mean an *entire* school locker, right in the room? What *kind* of car engine? An actual block of cement . . . You gotta give 'em credit for getting it in there.

What about the dishes? Sure, I guess the Smithsonian could figure out what was growing in them.

You know I came up with a really bizarre way to clean their rooms. You set fire to them. It's called a "contained blaze." You hire these guys who put out the oil spill fires to surround the room, then you toss in a match. Whoosh!!! The whole thing goes up, they put it out, and it's like a self-cleaning oven. All you've got to do is sweep out the ashes. Then you pass the room on to the next kid and you don't have to torch it for another three years.

Hey, I have to go. You've inspired me. I'm going in. Don't try to stop me. I promise I'll tie a rope around my waist like they did in *Poltergeist* so somebody can try to yank me out. If you don't hear from me tomorrow, THE ROOM won.

Hello—I'm trying to stay calm but I'm failing.

They're like walking X-rated scenes about to happen. The girls are Lolitas and the boys are . . . are . . . are men!!!

And we give them money and say, "Bye, have fun."

Why did we have children? Whose idea was this?

I don't want to be a grandmother. Especially to a child whose mother hasn't finished Solid Geometry.

Okay, okay, okay . . . I'm settling down. I know it'll be all right. We went through this same phase. We had the same urges. The same needs. BUT WE THOUGHT WE WERE SUPPOSED TO BE VIRGINS!!!!!!!!

I'm starting a movement to bring back virgins. You and I can be on the Board of Directors—it's made up of ex-virgins. We'll have virgin bylaws:

1. Sex before marriage is bad.
2. Sex when you're too young is bad.
3. Sex without love is bad.
4. Sex while your mother is alive is bad.

Remember the rallies for free speech, free love, and women burning their bras? Make love, not war. We weren't going to be uptight like our parents.

Well . . . WE WERE WRONG! Suddenly I'm worshipping at the altar of Pat Nixon. Did Julie and Tricia do things like this? Never! They had Secret Service agents threatening the boys they dated. "Son, you put your hand there and you're going to lose the use of an unnamed vital organ."

Why am I overreacting this way? I know we've raised good kids. At least you have. Personally I've failed miserably. Two kids just walked past me entwined like ivy growing up the side of Miss November and do you know what they said to me? "How's it hanging?"

I have to go now and turn out the light in my closet and sit there underneath my dresses in the darkness and pretend I'm six again. Bye.

Hi again.

I never even asked how you were holding up. Okay, I won't ask.

Did you ever think we'd make it this far with these kids? I somehow imagined I was always in high school. I mean, aren't you ALWAYS in high school in your memories?

So then, how can THEY be graduating from high school? I don't remember your child or mine in MY senior class.

I know it's a cliché but I have to say it at least once. WE'RE TOO YOUNG FOR THIS!!!

They're going to college. It's not enough that they shave, use deodorant (now and then), buy tampons, have deep voices, insist on all natural fabrics, and rarely have burping contests anymore but . . . GOING TO COLLEGE???

It's today. It really is. But it can't be. It can't be them going through this already when it seems like we just went through it ourselves. Putting on those robes and trying to figure out which side that dopey little tassel goes on. And wondering if you're supposed to wear anything under the robe and trying desperately to stay awake when the Chairman of the Board of International Boredom addresses the class about the promise of the future and blah-blah-blah-blah . . .

But it's not us.

It's them. Our children.

When they cross the stage and take that diploma I'll be fine. I'll just take a deep breath, close my eyes, make a mental picture of this wonderful moment . . . and weep uncontrollably for thirty or forty straight hours.

My baby's gone!!!!

Just when I was getting good at this mother stuff.

But, on the other hand, it does free up a whole room of the house.

Call you tomorrow . . . like always.